JUST BEING DALÍ

The Story of Artist Salvador Dalí

by
AMY GUGLIELMO

illustrated by
BRETT HELQUIST

putnam

G. P. Putnam's Sons

In a small seaside town on the northern edge of Spain lived a boy with big dreams and an even bigger name: Salvador Domingo Felipe Jacinto Dalí i Domènech.

As soon as he could walk, little Salvador wandered along the rocky shores near his home, chasing butterflies and birds. His chubby finger pointed to the sky, tracing puffy clouds as they shifted into prancing horses.

At six years old, Salvador yearned to be a cook.

But after one too many messes in the kitchen, his father gave him a pet bat to keep him occupied.

Then Salvador fancied being a king.
But his father was strict and soon grew
tired of all the pretending.
"Why can't you just behave?" he asked.

But Salvador was just **BEING HIMSELF.**

At school, Salvador didn't fit in. He was timid
and quiet and wanted to play alone. When he
wore his costume to class, the other kids teased
him and threw grasshoppers in his hair.

"Why are you so strange?" they asked.

But Salvador was only
BEING
HIMSELF

Salvador wasn't a serious student and he disliked being stuck inside. He found it more interesting to stare at the cracks on the ceiling, arranging the shapes into elephants and faces. He spent hours daydreaming out the window and filling his notebooks with doodles instead of schoolwork.

His teachers grew frustrated. "Why can't you act like the other students?"

But Salvador couldn't help BEING HIMSELF.

One day, Salvador fell ill. His parents sent him to the countryside to recover. There, he stayed with the family of artist Ramon Pichot. Salvador marveled at the vibrant paintings that dotted the walls, and when he grew stronger, Pichot taught him how to paint.

Suddenly, Salvador realized how he could truly be himself. Artists could be anything they liked. So he decided that's just what he would be.

When Salvador painted a pile of cherries and added real stems and worms to the canvas, Pichot persuaded Salvador's reluctant father to make him a studio.

Back at home, visions of a hillside kingdom danced from
Salvador's mind onto the walls of their old laundry room.

From then on, Salvador never stopped drawing.
He took classes and sketched everyone in his family.

And when he ran
out of people to draw,
he stood on his head
to spark new ideas.

A few years later, he was accepted to an art academy in Madrid.

At school, he grew his hair long and wore elegant outfits. The other students thought he was odd . . . until they were dazzled by his portfolio. Then he finally made some friends.

At first, Salvador threw himself into his studies. He worked tirelessly to master the techniques and to re-create the works of great artists.

But he soon grew tired of making art that looked like everyone else's. When Salvador was asked to reproduce a marble sculpture of a woman, he painted a picture of scales instead.

He challenged his professors and encouraged his classmates to do the same. Eventually, his rebellious behavior got him expelled. "Why can't you just follow the rules?" his instructors grumbled.

But Salvador kept BEING

HIMSELF.

More determined than ever, Salvador experimented with different styles. Using the techniques he had learned in school, combined with fantastic images from his dreams, he began creating paintings that were all his own.

Salvador moved to Paris, where he met a group of playful artists and writers who also united fantasy and reality in their works. At last, Salvador found others who thought and expressed themselves like he did. They called themselves surrealists.

The surrealists wanted people to think about art, rather than
just look at it. By placing objects in strange and unexpected
combinations, Salvador and the other surrealists grabbed
the attention of the critics and public alike.

Then Salvador caught the eye of Gala, the woman of his dreams, who didn't mind that he often made a scene. She adored how Salvador placed flowers in his hair and how he wore a cape, a curly mustache, and funny shoes. They fell in love, and Gala became his muse.

Despite his talent, Salvador had trouble selling his odd works of art. Back in Spain and nearly penniless, he and Gala moved into an old fishing shack by the sea.

One hot night after dinner, Salvador struggled with an unfinished landscape painting. Frustrated, he was about to leave the house when he spotted a plate of cheese that had melted into a blob. That gave him an idea.

Salvador painted watches, soft and runny, like cheese. He added swarming ants and a mysterious figure in a strange desert setting. He called it *The Persistence of Memory*.

When Gala came home, she was amazed. "I will never forget this painting!"

Would others agree?

Salvador and Gala traveled to America, where the new painting was displayed in a surrealist show in New York City. Though the painting was small—only a little larger than a sheet of paper—it was a sensation.

But what did it mean? People had many ideas.

"I think it's about how time is relative."

"I think it's about how memories fade."

"Maybe it's a self-portrait."

No one knew for sure. But everyone agreed: Salvador had painted a dream.

The Persistence of Memory became Salvador's masterpiece. When the iconic image found a home at the Museum of Modern Art in New York City, people flocked to see it. Salvador became the most famous artist of his time.

But soon Salvador's antics drew more attention than his art.
He drove a fancy car stuffed with one thousand pounds of cauliflower.

He gave a speech inside a deep-sea diving suit.

And he took his pet ocelot, Babou, to lunch at snooty restaurants.

Eventually, even the surrealists insisted he curb
his wild ways or leave their group.
"Why can't you be more like us?" they asked.

But Salvador wouldn't stop
BEING HIMSELF.

Salvador became famous for his eccentric and pioneering ways.
He designed lollipop wrappers in exchange for free candy,
a lobster phone that really worked, and a hat made out of a shoe!
He had little time for painting, as he was too busy appearing on
television and having parties.

The critics asked, *Why?*
"Why do you have to act outrageous?"
"What's the point of all this silly behavior?"
"Why do you do all these things?"
They told him, "Stick to art!"

But Salvador didn't mind . . .
And his fans didn't, either.

After all, he was just BEING HIMSELF.

Born in Figueres, Spain, in 1904, Salvador Dalí was a daydreamer and a storyteller from the start. As a child, he had an active imagination, and he was encouraged to make things by his creative mother. His father, however, had hoped that someday Dalí would become a lawyer like him.

Dalí was considered a talented art student, yet he was actually expelled from art school twice—once for leading a student protest, and again when he refused to complete his final exams.

In 1929, Dalí moved to Paris and joined an artistic and literary movement called surrealism, which was started by French poet André Breton. Dalí became friends with other surrealist artists such as Jean Arp, René Magritte, and Max Ernst, and through his new friends he met his wife, Gala, who served as his inspiration and the subject of many of his pieces. Dalí called her his queen, and even bought her a castle!

The surrealists were interested in art that explored the subconscious, or the part of the mind that we are not fully aware of. They believed they could access the subconscious through their dreams and by trying to write or draw automatically, without thinking. Dalí became obsessed with his dreams, and he even slept with a canvas next to his pillow so he could wake up and paint before he forgot them. He once said, "Give me two hours a day of activity, and I'll take the other twenty-two in dreams."

"I am not strange. I am just not normal."
—Salvador Dalí

In 1931, when he was just twenty-seven years old, Dalí painted one of the most famous works of surrealist art, *The Persistence of Memory*. Though there are several theories about the meaning of the painting, Dalí claimed that the work was inspired by a melted wheel of Camembert cheese.

Dalí was a controversial figure in his time, and he remains so today. While his fans couldn't wait to see what wild things he would make or do next, the surrealists grew annoyed with his increasingly sensationalist behavior. They thought he seemed more interested in publicity, fame, and money than creating serious art. In 1934, André Breton tried to expel Dalí with a "trial," but Dalí prevailed and remained with the group until 1939, when the surrealists finally expelled him for good.

Throughout his life, Dalí created more than 1,500 paintings, as well as sculptures, films, jewelry, furniture, window displays, and sets for ballets and plays. He even wrote a cookbook, a novel, and a book about his mustache! Many of his works now live in the Dalí Theatre-Museum, located in the same building in Figueres, Spain, where he had his first art show as a teenager.

SELECTED BIBLIOGRAPHY

Anderson, Robert. *Salvador Dalí*. London: Franklin Watts, 2002.

Goff, Robert, and Salvador Dalí. *The Essential Salvador Dalí*. New York: Harry N. Abrams, 1998.

Moorhouse, Paul, and Salvador Dalí. *Dalí*. San Diego: Thunder Bay Press, 1990.

Toyne, Jessica. *Dalí*. Broomall, PA: Mason Crest, 2016.

SOURCE NOTES

In *Just Being Dalí*, the dialogue was re-created and invented by the author. The quote "I will never forget this painting" comes from the following source: Moorhouse [p. 49].

WORKS OF ART FEATURED IN THIS BOOK

pg. 18–19[1] (clockwise from left):

René Magritte, *The Treachery of Images (This Is Not a Pipe)*, 1929, Los Angeles County Museum of Art, Los Angeles, CA, USA

Jean (Hans) Arp, *Untitled (Collage with Squares Arranged According to the Law of Chance)*, 1916–1917, Museum of Modern Art, New York, NY, USA

Max Ernst, *The Wheel of Light (La Roue de la lumière)* from *Natural History (Histoire naturelle)*, c. 1925, published 1926, Museum of Modern Art, New York, NY, USA

Jean (Hans) Arp, *Configuration*, 1927, Fine Arts Museum Basel, Basel, Switzerland

René Magritte, *The False Mirror*, 1929, Museum of Modern Art, New York, NY, USA

Man Ray, *Object to Be Destroyed*, 1923, destroyed in 1957

Max Ernst, *At the First Clear Word*, 1923, Art Collection North Rhine-Westphalia, Düsseldorf, Germany

Miró, Joan, *Painting [Blue]*, 1927, Private Collection

pg. 24–25, 26:

Salvador Dalí, *The Persistence of Memory*, 1931, Museum of Modern Art, New York, NY, USA

pg. 32–33 (from left):

Salvador Dalí, *Lobster Telephone*, 1936, Tate Modern, London, England

Elsa Schiaparelli collaboration with Salvador Dalí, *Hat*, 1937–1938, The Metropolitan Museum of Art, New York, NY, USA

Salvador Dalí, Chupa Chups logo, 1969

pg. 34–35 (clockwise from left):

Elsa Schiaparelli collaboration with Salvador Dalí, *Woman's Dinner Dress*, 1937, Philadelphia Museum of Art, Philadelphia, PA, USA

Salvador Dalí, *Sleep*, 1937, Private Collection

Salvador Dalí, *Meditative Rose*, 1958, Mr. and Mrs. Arnold Grant Collection, New York, NY, USA

Salvador Dalí, *Mae West Lips Sofa*, 1936, Dalí Theatre-Museum, Figueres, Catalonia, Spain

---

[1] Counting title page as page 1.

For my art mentors, especially Diane Fine —A. G.

For Richard Hull, a great teacher —B. H.

G. P. PUTNAM'S SONS

An imprint of Penguin Random House LLC, New York

Text copyright © 2021 by Amy Guglielmo

Illustrations copyright © 2021 by Brett Helquist

Visit us online at penguinrandomhouse.com

Library of Congress Cataloging-in-Publication Data
Names: Guglielmo, Amy, author. | Helquist, Brett, illustrator.
Title: Just being Dalí : the story of artist Salvador Dalí / by Amy Guglielmo; illustrated by Brett Helquist.
Description: New York: G. P. Putnam's Sons, [2021] | Includes bibliographical references. | Summary: "Salvador Dalí struggles to
follow the rules and fit in with his peers, until one day he realizes that artists can be and do anything they like.
This realization gives him the freedom to truly be himself"—Provided by publisher.
Identifiers: LCCN 2020012398 | ISBN 9781984816580 (hardcover) | ISBN 9781984816597 (ebook) |
ISBN 9781984816603 (kindle edition)
Subjects: LCSH: Dalí, Salvador, 1904–1989—Juvenile literature. | Artists—Spain—Biography—Juvenile literature.
Classification: LCC N7113.D3 G84 2021 | DDC 709.2 [B]—dc23
LC record available at https://lccn.loc.gov/2020012398

Manufactured in China by RR Donnelley Asia Printing Solutions Ltd.
ISBN 9781984816580
1 3 5 7 9 10 8 6 4 2

Design by Marikka Tamura
Text set in Baxter New Style
The art was done in oil on paper.